FOLLOWING JESUS
A NEW LIFE

Therefore, if anyone is in Christ, the new creation has come:
The old has gone, the new is here!
—2 Corinthians 5:17

The most important decision that you make in this life is deciding who you will follow. Who you follow determines the quality of life on earth and the life after. There is no greater life than the one lived following Jesus! It is a life where you lay down everything, only to find you have more than you ever had before.

One of the people who Jesus put in charge of the Church when it first began was a man named Paul. He had quite the impressive resume in life, but he didn't really experience fulfillment until he encountered Jesus and decided to follow him. This is what he said:

But whatever were gains to me I now consider loss for the sake of
Christ. What is more, I consider everything a loss because of the
surpassing worth of knowing Christ Jesus my Lord, for whose sake I
have lost all things. I consider them garbage, that I may gain Christ.
—Philippians 3:7-8

People are always looking for happiness and fulfillment, but only when we turn from our way to following Jesus will we walk in everything that he has for us! This is why the Bible is so specific about declaring Jesus as our Lord. It's not enough just to believe that he's real; you must choose to follow him.

WHAT'S NEXT?

As a follower of Jesus for many years now, I know firsthand the value of having someone help you learn to walk out your faith, which is why we created this book—to help with the essential beginning steps after choosing to follow Jesus.

The Bible is the exhaustive book on following Jesus, and this book is designed to be a quick guide to your next seven essential steps in your walk with him. Each chapter will break down one of the key things you need to know and show you how to do it. At the end of each chapter you'll see additional verses you can use if you'd like to study the topic through further.

Before we get into those steps, I want to talk about a foundational truth regarding the heart and character of God that the entire Bible and your relationship with Jesus are built on.

"GOD LOVES YOU AND WANTS TO BE CLOSE TO YOU."

As you develop your relationship with God, it's important to know he isn't tolerating you, or putting up with you, or trying to get rid of you; he has done everything to be close to you. God loves us and wants to be with us. When we sinned, he couldn't stay away; he wants a relationship with us for all eternity. *He's not satisfied with a distant association; he wants to be close to us.*

From the beginning of time, God walked with the people that he loves, as he did when he spent time with Adam and Eve in the Garden of Eden. But, because God loved them, he also gave them a choice to love him back. Even in that perfect garden, they chose to disobey God and sin. After sin created a gap between God and humanity, God's plan to bring us back to himself was set into motion, which is embodied in this iconic verse:

For God so loved the world that he gave his one and only Son, that whoever believes in him shall not perish but have eternal life.
—John 3:16

God could have stayed away, but instead he cut through everything to be with us. Before Jesus came, God's presence was experienced only by the High Priest when he went behind the veil into what was called the Most Holy Place. This veil represented a separation between humanity and God. As you can imagine, God wasn't about that! Let the full reality and emotion of the next verse

2

CONTENTS

FOLLOWING JESUS | A NEW LIFE   1

CHAPTER 1 | PRAYER & WORSHIP   6

CHAPTER 2 | THE BIBLE   14

CHAPTER 3 | WATER BAPTISM   24

CHAPTER 4 | THE HOLY SPIRIT   28

CHAPTER 5 | THE CHURCH   35

CHAPTER 6 | SHARING YOUR FAITH   41

CHAPTER 7 | LOVING PEOPLE   49

IT'S YOUR TURN   53

FOLLOWING JESUS EXTRAS   58

CHAPTER ANSWER KEY   59

FOLLOWINGJESUSBOOK.COM

Come close to God, and God will come close to you.

–James 4:8 (NLT)

hit you as you realize God's heart to eliminate anything that would come between us:

And when Jesus had cried out again in a loud voice, he gave up his spirit. At that moment the curtain of the temple was torn in two from top to bottom.
—Matthew 27:50-51

AT THAT MOMENT! How amazing is that? The first possible moment God had to be close to us, he took it. He made a strong statement to everyone—*all* were now welcome to come to him. Later, one of the great leaders of the Church wrote one of my favorite verses in the Bible:

Come close to God, and God will come close to you.
—James 4:8 (NLT)

Through Jesus, we now are able to come close to God again. The sin and brokenness that held us back and away from God are now taken care of by Jesus. The Bible says that the cost of sin is death. There is a price that has to be paid, and through the perfect sacrifice of Jesus that debt is satisfied.

The Bible says that Jesus was a "ransom for many" (Matthew 20:28; Mark 10:45). I love the word *ransom*; it means to aggressively take back. Sin had found us held captive by the devil and a slave to his ways, but Jesus left heaven, came to earth, and with his death on the cross, he ransomed us; he took us back from the control of the enemy to be close to himself again.

In the final book of the Bible, we see another example of God's desire to be close to us with this open invitation by Jesus:

Here I am! I stand at the door and knock. If anyone hears my voice and opens the door, I will come in and eat with that person, and they with me.
—Revelation 3:20

As you follow Jesus, never forget how much he loves you and wants to be close to you. Jesus' invitation isn't based on our perfection or our ability to do all the right things. It is because of the *grace* of Jesus that this invitation to come close was made available.

More than anything, I pray that this book will encourage you to come close to God!

HAVE YOU DECIDED?

Before continuing, I want to give you an opportunity to answer the question, "Who is the leader of your life?" If you've already declared Jesus as that leader, that is awesome! Get into the book! If not, then why wait? In Romans 10:9-10 it says that if we declare that Jesus is Lord, we will be saved. If you're ready to go all in and follow Jesus, begin with this passionate prayer:

"Jesus, thank you for dying on the cross for my sins, and rising from the dead to give me life. I repent of my sin and turn to you. Today I choose to follow you with all of my heart, for the rest of my life. I believe in you and declare that you are the leader and Lord of my life! Thank you for forgiving me and walking with me from this moment forward! Amen."

FOLLOWING JESUS EXTRAS

Discover all that God has for you with our complimentary video guides and devotionals.
FOLLOWINGJESUSBOOK.COM/EXTRAS

CHAPTER CHALLENGE

STUDY IT THROUGH:
Here are several key verses that walk you through an overview of
God's Creation and the ultimate salvation of humanity.

God Created Us:
Genesis 1:27; Psalm 139:13-14

God Loves Us:
Jeremiah 31:3; John 3:16; 1 John 3:1

Our Sin/Disobedience:
Genesis 3; Romans 3:23; 6:23

Jesus' Sacrifice/Cross:
Luke 9:22; Hebrews 9:22; 1 Peter 3:18

Our Decision/Repentance:
Romans 10:9-13; Acts 16:29-31

His Grace/Forgiveness:
Ephesians 2:8-9; Romans 5:1-2

Life in Christ; Following Jesus:
John 10:10; Romans 8:37-39; Matthew 5:16; Luke 9:23

His Kingdom; the Church:
Ephesians 1:17-23; Matthew 6:33; 1 Corinthians 12:12-31

Heaven; Eternity:
John 14:1-6; Hebrews 4:14; Philippians 3:20; 2 Corinthians 5:7-10

CHAPTER 1

PRAYER & WORSHIP

Rejoice always, pray continually, give thanks in all circumstances;
for this is God's will for you in Christ Jesus.
—1 Thessalonians 5:16-18

The Christian life is not just about knowing and doing; it's about *being with Jesus.* Before we focus on any specific practices, habits, or spiritual routines, we must realize following Jesus begins simply by spending *time* with Jesus.

How much time? The answer cannot be reduced down to rules needing to be followed. For example, what if I tell a husband that the best way to get to know his wife is to spend time with her, and he asks, "How much time do I have to spend with her?" That response would be considered rude and too mechanical for a relationship.

Not only do we need to spend time with God to grow our relationship, but incredibly, that is what he desires as well! God wants to spend time with us.

Not only is spending time with Jesus the way we develop our relationship with him, but at our very core we are designed for relationship with our Father and Creator. Without him, we live a subpar life and will be constantly chasing other things for fulfillment.

We are designed to know, love, walk with, and worship God. While Jesus was on the earth, someone asked him, "What is the greatest commandment?" We read about this and his response in Matthew:

"Teacher, which is the greatest commandment in the Law?" Jesus
replied: "Love the Lord your God with all your heart and with all
your soul and with all your mind."
—Matthew 22:36-37

The greatest priority is to love God with all that we have. If God isn't the center of our life, our worship, and our work, nothing will make sense. Everything flows more effectively once we put Jesus as the primary focus of our lives. There's another story from the Bible that shows this primary importance of spending time with Jesus in Luke 10:

As Jesus and his disciples were on their way, he came to a village where a woman named Martha opened her home to him. She had a sister called Mary, who sat at the Lord's feet listening to what he said. But Martha was distracted by all the preparations that had to be made. She came to him and asked, "Lord, don't you care that my sister has left me to do the work by myself? Tell her to help me!" "Martha, Martha," the Lord answered, "you are worried and upset about many things, but few things are needed—or indeed only one. Mary has chosen what is better, and it will not be taken away from her."
—Luke 10:38-42

It's important to notice that Jesus says only one thing is needed; he elevates spending time with him as our highest pursuit. This should be the priority and focus of our lives. Often, like Martha, we find ourselves distracted and pulled away, but the most important thing is to spend time with Jesus.

With that being said, how do we do this? What does it mean to "spend time with Jesus," since he is no longer physically walking the earth? We spend time with God through prayer, worship, Bible reading, and the Holy Spirit. In this chapter we will focus on prayer and worship.

PRAYER

One of the best ways to view prayer is to see it as talking with God. It's a conversation that goes both ways; you talk to God and God talks to you. Through prayer we have access to his presence and power. So many Christians settle for less than what God wants for them, because they don't take time to pray.

HEARING THE VOICE OF GOD

One of the most important questions—and often the most common—is, "How do I hear God when he talks?" One of my favorite Scriptures that give us a clue how to do this is found in 1 Samuel:

> *The boy Samuel ministered before the LORD under Eli. In those days the word of the LORD was rare; there were not many visions. One night Eli, whose eyes were becoming so weak that he could barely see, was lying down in his usual place. The lamp of God had not yet gone out, and Samuel was lying down in the house of the LORD, where the ark of God was. Then the LORD called Samuel.*
> —1 Samuel 3:1-4

You see in these few verses that Samuel positioned himself in a place where God could speak to him. Often we find ourselves like Eli in this story—distracted, busy, and away from God's presence. Can God shout over the noise of our lives? Yes, but he usually asks us to quiet our lives and lean in to hear his voice.

I've found that the more time I spend talking and listening to God, the more I am able to discern if God is speaking to me or not. It's similar to how we have the ability to pick out the voice of our parent or child from a distance. Because we've spent enough time with them, we recognize their voice over the other voices.

> *My sheep listen to my voice; I know them, and they follow me.*
> —John 10:27

When you spend time with God, pray; talk to God, then take time to listen and write down what you feel like you hear him saying. God may choose to talk to you in an audible voice, but usually he speaks to us in our spirit. So, you don't hear him with your ears, you hear him with your spirit. Sometimes he'll want to give you specific instructions about something or he may just want to reaffirm his love for you!

Knowing what the Bible says is a huge clue to learning how to recognize when God is speaking to you. God will never say anything to you that contradicts his Word. In the beginning stages of following

Jesus, if you feel God is telling you to do something extreme, I highly recommend that you share it with a more mature Christian. They will be able to help you process it, so you don't make a wrong move out of immaturity. But, if God is speaking to you, act on it quickly and fully!

"PRAYER IS THE GREATEST PRIVILEGE OF HUMANITY."

God also calls us to pray on behalf of his will on earth. The first purpose of prayer is to grow our relationship with God, but that isn't all. God calls us to devote ourselves to prayer. The Bible says that the prayer of the righteous person is powerful and effective. God chooses to work through his Spirit and our prayers.

In Ezekiel 22, God was looking for someone to stand in the gap on behalf of a city so that it could be saved, but sadly, it says he found no one.

I looked for someone among them who would build up the wall and stand before me in the gap on behalf of the land so I would not have to destroy it, but I found no one.
—Ezekiel 22:30

God is looking for you and me to stand in the gap and pray for individuals, cities, and countries. The kingdom of God advances on the prayers of his people. Don't assume that our prayers don't matter or that they won't do much. Actually, it's the opposite; our prayers are powerful and essential for the work of God to move forward. When Jesus walked the earth, he first called twelve disciples to follow him. They once asked Jesus to teach them how to pray; here is what he said:

And when you pray, do not be like the hypocrites, for they love to pray standing in the synagogues and on the street corners to be seen by others. Truly I tell you, they have received their reward in full. But when you pray, go into your room, close the door and pray to your Father, who is unseen. Then your Father, who sees what is done in secret, will reward you. And when you pray, do not keep on babbling like pagans, for they think they will be heard because of their many words. Do not be like them, for your Father knows what you need before you ask him. This, then, is how you should pray: "Our Father in heaven, hallowed be

9

your name, your kingdom come, your will be done, on earth as it is in heaven. Give us today our daily bread. And forgive us our debts, as we also have forgiven our debtors. And lead us not into temptation, but deliver us from the evil one."
—Matthew 6:5-13

There are many great studies on these few verses that Jesus gives us on prayer, but let me give a few thoughts to help us quickly take away what Jesus wants us to see.

Approach Is Important: (Our Father, You Are Holy)
When you pray, come to God in awe and reverence of his greatness and the fact that he is a loving Father. It is important to give him the honor that he deserves, because how you see God will determine your ability to have faith for him to respond. If you see God as small, you'll pray small; if you see him as the Almighty and All-Sufficient One, you'll pray bigger and expect more!

Put His Purpose First: (Your Will Be Done)
Many people come to God begging and only asking for what they want, rather than partnering with God in prayer for his will to be done on earth. If you pray for the advancement of God's will, you'll also find that God takes care of your needs and wants.

Make a Request: (Give Us Our Daily Bread)
Never be shy about asking God for what you need. He loves to provide and respond to our requests. Jesus says we don't have because we don't ask.

Forgive Us: (Forgive as We Forgive)
It is so important that we realize how much we've been forgiven, so that we continue to release forgiveness to others. Confess your own sins quickly and be quick to offer forgiveness to others when they wrong you.

Protect and Lead Us: (Lead Us, Deliver Us)
God wants to lead our lives, but he doesn't force his way in. He looks for us to lean in and ask. He wants us to pursue him and walk with him.

Your Father and Savior cannot wait for the next time you stop and spend time with him. Don't limit prayer to mealtimes and church buildings. God wants to hear from you every day. Your world desperately needs you to stand in the gap and pray for his will to be done on earth!

WORSHIP

One of my favorite ways to spend time with God is through worship. If you want to experience the presence of God, begin to worship. A key part of my prayer times usually includes listening to worship music, singing, and lifting up the name of Jesus! One of the greatest warriors and worshipers in the Bible was King David. I love his heart for worship:

Shout for joy to the LORD, all the earth. Worship the LORD with gladness; come before him with joyful songs. Know that the LORD is God. It is he who made us, and we are his; we are his people, the sheep of his pasture. Enter his gates with thanksgiving and his courts with praise; give thanks to him and praise his name. For the LORD is good and his love endures forever; his faithfulness continues through all generations.
—Psalm 100:1-5

Worship aligns our heart to his. It creates a landing pad for the presence of God in our life. Like a helicopter that looks for the H to land on, worship puts a neon target on our life that invites the presence and power of God to land.

In times of worship, we'll often have a heightened sense of the presence of God, but worship is not just a response to good feelings or only something we do when we feel like it. Worship is what we do regardless of circumstances or feelings. Often, taking a few moments in worship to lift up your hands and sing will greatly impact your life and the climate of your heart.

LEAD WITH WORSHIP

Alongside prayer, worship has a powerful dual nature to it. On one hand it creates the perfect atmosphere to connect with God, and on the other, it is also used as a way to fight against the work of the enemy.

After consulting the people, Jehoshaphat appointed men to sing to the Lord and to praise him for the splendor of his holiness as they went out at the head of the army, saying: "Give thanks to the Lord, for his love endures forever." As they began to sing and praise, the Lord set ambushes against the men of Ammon and Moab and Mount Seir who were invading Judah, and they were defeated.
—2 Chronicles 20:21-22

No matter what you're facing, lead with worship! As the men in this passage worshipped, God began to work. In your life, when you're facing a difficult situation, stop, take time to worship God, and watch him begin to move in your situation. Worship is potent; it releases the power of God and it calms and quiets your heart so that you can hear God speak to you.

CHAPTER CHALLENGE

STUDY IT THROUGH:

What does the Bible say about prayer and thankfulness? 1 Thessalonians 5:16-18

_____

What does God ask us to pray for? Psalm 2:8

_____

How should we pray? Luke 18:1-8

_____

What does Jesus say about fasting? Matthew 6:16-18

_____

Who are we to worship? Luke 4:8

_____

What does Psalm 96:1-10 say that the Lord is worthy of?

_____

WALK IT OUT:

- Set time aside daily to pray.
- Pray for 15 minutes at a time and slowly increase the length.
- Create a worship playlist and worship God outside of a church service.
- Pray for others and for God's grace on your city.

CHAPTER 2

THE BIBLE

Your word is a lamp for my feet, a light on my path.
—Psalm 119:105

Wouldn't it be great if we just had a direct way to hear from God and he'd give us a manual to live by? The good news is, that's exactly what the Bible is. If you've heard of the Bible, but never really read it, you may not realize how incredible it is. God's Word is the greatest book, filled with the best practices for humanity.

When we apply the principles, practices, and commands in the Bible, our lives will grow, advance, and thrive in every way. But, even more than that, the Bible is the very Word of God. It's his presence and his heart. God won't love you more if you read the Bible and he won't love you less if you don't. You don't read the Bible because you have to; you read the Bible knowing that it is God's Word and heart for us directly.

The Bible:
The Bible reveals who God is.
The Bible shows us who we are.
The Bible lays out our purpose.

GOD WANTS TO SPEAK TO YOU

When I read the Bible it reminds me of who God says I am. As a father, I often tell my daughters that it doesn't matter what anyone else says, they just need to remember what I say about them. In the same way, when the world or even your own thoughts try to destroy you, just go back to the Book. Remember what God says about you.

Have patience with the process of growing new thoughts and habits. This is often one of the biggest challenges that many people face as they try to follow Jesus. They say, "Well I tried that and it didn't work." Usually when someone says this, it means they became impatient while waiting for the results or the "crop" to grow.

OUR LIVES NEED ALIGNMENT

Often a car will get out of alignment and the vehicle begins to shake as it drives, which can cause a lot of damage. The reality is, that because of sin, our lives are out of alignment. The way we get our life to stop "shaking" is to realign it to God's way of doing things, which we find in the Bible. Often in the world we live in, people want to alter the Bible to fit their life, rather than altering their life to align with the Word of God. The Bible talks about this in Romans 12:

Do not conform to the pattern of this world, but be transformed by the renewing of your mind. Then you will be able to test and approve what God's will is—his good, pleasing and perfect will.
—Romans 12:2

The world has a pattern and God has a pattern. Our life will function best and find the greatest fulfillment when we follow God's pattern. It's important to understand that this realignment process takes time. It's a process of transformation through the renewing of our minds, enabling us to think the way God thinks.

One of the challenging things for new Christians is that even though they've made a decision to follow Jesus, they feel like nothing is getting better like they expected it would. They are experiencing the process of being transformed.

The quality of our life is basically the result of the quality of our thoughts and how we act on those thoughts. As we read the Word of God and apply it to our life, the way we think and act will slowly become more like the way Jesus thinks and acts. That is when we see our life transformed. It's rarely an overnight "fix"; it is usually a process of changing over time.

Aligning our life to God's Word is not just about coming to a church gathering on Sunday; it's about our *whole* life. When Jesus calls us to follow him, we aren't just joining a club; we are choosing a new leader for our life.

FOLLOWING THE BIBLE

One of the primary indicators of our love and gratefulness for what Jesus has done for us is our obedience to his Word. We can't say we love Jesus but then disobey what he says. Our whole life must come into obedience with his Word.

We will never experience the life that God has for us if we limit following Jesus to the "Sunday Morning Church Box." Attending church services is an essential part of maturing as a follower of Christ, but we must follow Jesus Monday through Saturday as well. Allow God's Word to set the standard for every area of your life. Begin with the following Bible verses:

FAITH
Jesus replied: "'Love the Lord your God with all your heart and with all your soul and with all your mind.' This is the first and greatest commandment."
—Matthew 22:37-38

RELATIONSHIPS
Do nothing out of selfish ambition or vain conceit. Rather, in humility value others above yourselves, not looking to your own interests but each of you to the interests of the others.
—Philippians 2:3-4

MONEY
For the love of money is a root of all kinds of evil. Some people, eager for money, have wandered from the faith and pierced themselves with many griefs.
—1 Timothy 6:10

PARENTING
A rod and a reprimand impart wisdom, but a child left undisciplined disgraces its mother.
—Proverbs 29:15

SEXUALITY

It is God's will that you should be sanctified: that you should avoid
sexual immorality; that each of you should learn to control your own
body in a way that is holy and honorable, not in passionate lust like the
pagans, who do not know God.
—1 Thessalonians 4:3-5

WORK

Lazy hands make for poverty, but diligent hands bring wealth.
—Proverbs 10:4

These verses are just a few examples of how Scripture speaks and directs us in every area of our life. Following Jesus requires that we often exchange our opinions or the opinions from our culture to obey God's Word, but along with that is the most fulfilling and rewarding life.

Peter and the other apostles replied: "We must obey God rather
than human beings!"
—Acts 5:29

GOD'S WILL IS IN HIS WORD

One of the major questions all humanity wrestles with is trying to determine what God's will is for their life: What does God want me to do? There are many who have attempted to answer these major questions on their own, but if you try to discover your purpose outside of God you'll come up empty every time.

The great news is that God does give humanity some big-picture purpose statements. These directions can guide the larger boundaries of our lives. Sometimes God will speak very specifically, but most of the time he leaves daily decisions up to us and invites us to partner with him.

If you're wondering what your purpose is, begin with the instructions from God's Word to all humanity and work from there. If what you are doing isn't accomplishing the statements below, then you're not fulfilling your purpose.

1. FOR RELATIONSHIP WITH GOD

Why do we exist? Why were we created? If we don't have these questions answered, we have no foundation to build our lives on. Only followers of Jesus have the answers, as is highlighted in this verse:

For from him and through him and for him are all things. To him be the glory forever! Amen.
—Romans 11:36

We exist first and foremost to have relationship with God and to live a life that brings glory to him. Rest in the knowledge that you are loved and valued by God.

2. TO MULTIPLY WHAT YOU'RE GIVEN

God gave us life and he commissions us to do the same. This verse in the beginning of Genesis sets the stage for one of the primary purposes of humanity:

God blessed them and said to them, "Be fruitful and increase in number; fill the earth and subdue it. Rule over the fish in the sea and the birds in the sky and over every living creature that moves on the ground."
—Genesis 1:28

The Bible says that the earth is the Lord's and part of our purpose is to steward and manage it. Yes, taking care of planet earth is a God-given mandate. This doesn't mean we're not supposed to touch it or use it; the Bible encourages us to use all of its resources. God also expects us to improve on everything he gives us. Practically, this means caring for the world that we've been given: the workplace, family, community, country, and every area of life. Multiply and grow what you've been given.

3. TO EXTEND LOVE TO EVERYONE

This verse below reaffirms our primary purpose to love God and be in relationship with him, but it also gives us another primary mandate from heaven:

Jesus replied: "'Love the Lord your God with all your heart and with all your soul and with all your mind.' This is the first and greatest commandment. And the second is like it: 'Love your neighbor as yourself.'"
—Matthew 22:37-39

Love your neighbor! This is huge! Most of the time it's easy, but rarely do we get along with everyone. Because Jesus unconditionally loves us and gave his life for us, God requires that we forgive others who wrong us and love all people as an extension of the love we've been shown.

4. TO PRIORITIZE GOD'S KINGDOM

While God put us in charge of the earth, God still has an ultimate plan and purpose that he is working out on the earth, and he calls us to make that our primary focus as well:

But seek first his kingdom and his righteousness, and all these things will be given to you as well.
—Matthew 6:33

Too often we think as individuals disconnected from a greater plan. Now as a follower of Jesus, we're called to make *his* kingdom *our* purpose. Our personal life, our family, our work, our gifting, and our ministry should all revolve around how to best advance the Kingdom of God on earth.

5. TO SHARE THE GOOD NEWS

In the original plan for humanity in the Garden, everyone was in relationship with God and loved him, but after humanity sinned it caused a separation between us and God. Because God will not settle for being distant from us, he has given us a key mission while on earth—to share with everyone the salvation from our sins that is available through Jesus:

> *Therefore go and make disciples of all nations, baptizing them in the name of the Father and of the Son and of the Holy Spirit, and teaching them to obey everything I have commanded you. And surely I am with you always, to the very end of the age.*
> —Matthew 28:19-20

We'll talk more at length about this later in the book, but it's important to note that this isn't an option; it is a command of Jesus. This doesn't mean that everyone is supposed to become a preacher, but we all need to lead as many people to Jesus as we possibly can in our lifetime.

When we filter all of our life with the above key purposes of humanity in mind, we'll live with more of God's blessing on what we do, and we'll live fulfilled, knowing that our life has meaning and is a part of God's greater plan for the earth.

HOW TO READ THE BIBLE

I believe the best way to read the Bible, so you maximize its value, is to use an annual reading plan connected with the Bible study approach using the acronym S.O.A.P.

First, you'll want to select a Bible reading plan. I'd recommend a plan that has you read through the whole Bible in a year. My favorite is a one-year plan called *Life Journal Reading Plan.* This is available on the Bible App (which is what I use) or you may purchase the journal if you prefer the physical paper method. It's a great plan that will take you through the Old Testament once and the New Testament twice in the course of a year. It usually has a couple of chapters from the Old Testament, a Psalm/Proverb, and a chapter from the New Testament. You'll love it! As you read daily, use this acronym to help you apply God's Word to your life.

S = SCRIPTURE

As you're reading, look for one verse that really sticks out to you. If a verse jumps out to me, I will circle the verse number or copy the verse off my phone and paste it into my notes, so I can go back to it later. After you're done reading, either write the one verse at the top of your page or paste it into your page.

O = OBSERVATION

Now it's time to take a few moments to write down your observations about that specific verse. What do you see? What do you feel God saying to you about it? What seems to be the point of the verse?

A = APPLICATION

Now, write down how you're going to apply this to your life. Ask yourself, "How will I be different after reading this verse?"

P = PRAYER

Write out a prayer to God for the day and relate it to the verse you've just been reading.

SCRIPTURE MEMORIZATION

Memorizing Bible verses is not something that you have to do, but I highly encourage it. David said in Psalm 119.11, "*I have hidden your word in my heart that I might not sin against you.*"

Having key verses from the Bible committed to memory is powerful. When the pressures of life or the attack of the enemy try to come against you, you'll have the firepower of God's Word to fight against it.

Don't worry about having to try and memorize the whole Bible!! Instead, as you read and come across verses that stand out to you, write them down and commit them to memory.

STAY CONSISTENT

I'll finish this chapter by saying that I've been reading and applying the Bible for decades and I still get excited to read it every day. The more you spend time in the Word of God, the more you'll love it! And the more you apply it, the more you'll see your life transformed. Ultimately, as you read the Bible, you'll deepen your relationship with God beyond what you can imagine.

CHAPTER CHALLENGE

STUDY IT THROUGH:
What does Hebrews 4:12 and 2 Timothy 3:16 say the Bible is?

What does 2 Timothy 3:16-17 say the Bible is used for?

What does Psalm 119:130 say that the Word of God brings into your life?

How do we live a pure life? Psalm 119:9

What does Psalm 119:4 say about God's commands?

WALK IT OUT:
- Begin a reading plan this week.
- Ask, "How will I be different?" after each time you read.
- Memorize one verse.

CHAPTER 3

WATER BAPTISM

Therefore go and make disciples of all nations, baptizing them in the name of the Father and of the Son and of the Holy Spirit.
—Matthew 28:19

One of the first things that Jesus did as he was beginning his years of ministry was to get water baptized. When we get saved and become a follower of Jesus, this is one of the first things we should do as well. Deciding to follow Jesus is truly an internal heart decision, but water baptism is a public declaration of our faith in Jesus.

Water baptism is also a symbolic act of aligning yourself with Jesus' death, burial, and resurrection. When we go under the water, we identify with his death, and when we come out of the water, we identify with being raised up to new life like Jesus was.

"BAPTISM IS REPENTANCE AND SURRENDER."

Having been buried with him in baptism, in which you were also raised with him through faith in the powerful working of God, who raised him from the dead.
—Colossians 2:12 (ESV)

For as many of you as were baptized into Christ have put on Christ.
—Galatians 3:27 (ESV)

It is important that water baptism is not viewed as just a Christian ritual. Let's read a few verses from Romans 6 that give us a better understanding of what water baptism means and why it's such a powerful decision:

What shall we say, then? Shall we go on sinning so that grace may increase? By no means! We are those who have died to sin; how can we live in it any longer? Or don't you know that all of us who were baptized into Christ Jesus were baptized into his death? We were therefore buried with him through baptism into death in order that, just as Christ was raised from the dead through the glory of the Father, we too may live a new life.
—Romans 6:1-4

Baptism is a declaration that we are dying to our old way of living and taking on the new life of Jesus. We won't be perfect or get it all exactly right, but our goal is to leave the sin and disobedience of our past behind, and make honoring God and his Word our pursuit.

Some try to follow Jesus without giving up their past life of sin. As a follower of Jesus I cannot go on sinning and doing whatever I want or whatever I think feels right. As a Christian, God's thoughts, his Word, and his direction must be moved to the forefront of my daily decisions.

When Jesus called his disciples, they left everything in order to follow him. When we follow Jesus, we are submitting and surrendering to him as the Lord of our life.

While God does choose to partner with humanity to achieve his will and usually allows us the freedom to do it the way we enjoy, ultimately, we must remember that we are following and serving God. If my way is ever in conflict with God's way, I now choose to follow his way.

GETTING WATER BAPTIZED

Some reading this may have grown up in a church where they had water sprinkled on their head as a baby. However, when the Bible speaks of water baptism, it is referring to being fully submerged under water to identify with the death and resurrection of Jesus. When Jesus was a child his parents took him to be dedicated, but he wasn't water baptized until later in life. Similarly, if you were dedicated or had water sprinkled on you as a child, that's great, but water baptism is an important personal decision that you make when you're mature enough to choose to follow Jesus.

Your next step is to connect with someone at your church to find out how to participate in the next water baptism opportunity or to set up a time to be water baptized. This is an exciting and powerful step in following Jesus!

CHAPTER CHALLENGE

STUDY IT THROUGH:

What did Jesus do before he began his public ministry? Matthew 3:13-16

What are the two things we're called to do in response to the gospel? What will we receive? Acts 2:38

What accompanies believing? Mark 16:16

When we are water baptized, who does Jesus say that we should be baptized in the name of? Matthew 28:19

WALK IT OUT:
- If you haven't yet been baptized, reach out to your local church and schedule a time to be baptized.
- Invite all of your family and friends to join you for this water baptism.

CHAPTER 4

THE HOLY SPIRIT

*I am going to send you what my Father has promised; but stay in
the city until you have been clothed with power from on high.*
—Luke 24:49

You won't be able to experience the full presence of God on
earth apart from the Holy Spirit. The calling that God has for you is
designed with the power of the Holy Spirit in mind. Take a look at
one of the first things that the apostle Paul asks a new group of Jesus
followers:

*[Paul] asked them, "Did you receive the Holy Spirit when you
believed?" They answered, "No, we have not even heard that there is
a Holy Spirit." So Paul asked, "Then what baptism did you receive?"
"John's baptism," they replied. Paul said, "John's baptism was a baptism
of repentance. He told the people to believe in the one coming after
him, that is, in Jesus." On hearing this, they were baptized in the name
of the Lord Jesus. When Paul placed his hands on them, the Holy Spirit
came on them, and they spoke in tongues and prophesied.*
—Acts 19:2-6

Don't attempt to follow Jesus and achieve your purpose apart
from the Spirit of God. It may be surprising to you that Jesus himself
said to the disciples that it's better that he go away:

*But very truly I tell you, it is for your good that I am going away.
Unless I go away, the Advocate will not come to you; but if I go, I will
send him to you.*
—John 16:7

Jesus is saying, "I want to be with you and strengthen you," but because He had taken on the restraints of humanity He could only be in one place at one time. So he said, "If I go, I can send my Spirit to live with everyone, everywhere. There is nothing more comforting, and embracing than the presence of God through the Holy Spirit."

There are two primary functions of the Holy Spirit. The Holy Spirit is there for closeness and for power. First let's talk about closeness. I've spoken to this concept throughout this book; God wants to be close to us. This next verse talks about the fellowship of the Holy Spirit:

May the grace of the Lord Jesus Christ, and the love of God, and the fellowship of the Holy Spirit be with you all.
—2 Corinthians 13:14

God wants fellowship, which is both friendship and partnership. As you invite God to fill you with his Spirit, you'll receive a great sense of the presence of God and his love for you.

The other central function of the Holy Spirit is to provide power to accomplish your calling, which plays a part in God's larger plan on earth. Here is what Jesus told the disciples before he left earth:

On one occasion, while he was eating with them, he gave them this command: "Do not leave Jerusalem, but wait for the gift my Father promised, which you have heard me speak about. For John baptized with water, but in a few days you will be baptized with the Holy Spirit. . . . But you will receive power when the Holy Spirit comes on you; and you will be my witnesses in Jerusalem, and in all Judea and Samaria, and to the ends of the earth."
—Acts 1:4-5, 8

You will receive power to be a witness for Jesus. As you begin to walk with the Holy Spirit, he'll speak to you and empower you to be a witness in what you say and do.

When the day of Pentecost came, they were all together in one place. Suddenly a sound like the blowing of a violent wind came from heaven and filled the whole house where they were sitting. They saw what

seemed to be tongues of fire that separated and came to rest on each of them. All of them were filled with the Holy Spirit and began to speak in other tongues as the Spirit enabled them.
—Acts 2:1-4

WALK BY THE HOLY SPIRIT

The Holy Spirit being able to be in and fill each believer is the total fulfillment of God's desire to be Immanuel—God with us. While we live on earth, we have access to the Holy Spirit. He wants to provide wisdom, counsel, power, comfort, direction, and friendship.

When we learn to follow the leading of the Holy Spirit, we're more fulfilled and more effective. The Holy Spirit also guides us in living a life that honors God. Here are a few verses describing what our lives begin to produce as we follow the Spirit versus our own way:

So I say, walk by the Spirit, and you will not gratify the desires of the flesh. For the flesh desires what is contrary to the Spirit, and the Spirit what is contrary to the flesh. They are in conflict with each other, so that you are not to do whatever you want. But if you are led by the Spirit, you are not under the law. The acts of the flesh are obvious: sexual immorality, impurity and debauchery; idolatry and witchcraft; hatred, discord, jealousy, fits of rage, selfish ambition, dissensions, factions and envy; drunkenness, orgies, and the like. I warn you, as I did before, that those who live like this will not inherit the kingdom of God. But the fruit of the Spirit is love, joy, peace, forbearance, kindness, goodness, faithfulness, gentleness and self-control. Against such things there is no law. Those who belong to Christ Jesus have crucified the flesh with its passions and desires. Since we live by the Spirit, let us keep in step with the Spirit.
—Galatians 5:16-25

If we're going to follow Jesus, we have to learn to listen and obey the voice and leading of the Holy Spirit. Jesus leads us through his Word and his Spirit. As we walk in step with the Holy Spirit, we'll begin to display the fruit of the Spirit that Galatians 5 showcases for us.

SUPERNATURAL POWER

You may have heard about or already experienced the supernatural power of God. All of this is done through the power of the Holy Spirit working through humans.

In ourselves, we don't have the power to heal people or set them free from oppression, but when we are filled with the Holy Spirit, there is a power that is now available to us. Even Jesus didn't do miracles until he was water baptized and the Holy Spirit came on him:

You know what has happened throughout the province of Judea, beginning in Galilee after the baptism that John preached—how God anointed Jesus of Nazareth with the Holy Spirit and power, and how he went around doing good and healing all who were under the power of the devil, because God was with him.
—Acts 10:37-38

The world that you and I live in is hurting and desperately in need of the love and power of God. This is why he wants to empower you with his Spirit—to bring life everywhere you go.

BEING FILLED WITH THE HOLY SPIRIT

When they arrived, they prayed for the new believers there that they might receive the Holy Spirit, because the Holy Spirit had not yet come on any of them; they had simply been baptized in the name of the Lord Jesus. Then Peter and John placed their hands on them, and they received the Holy Spirit.
—Acts 8:15-17

Being filled with the Holy Spirit as a young teenager became the game changer in my ability to know and follow Jesus. In most biblical accounts, believers received the Holy Spirit when someone laid hands on them. There were also reports of people getting filled as they simply heard God's Word spoken.

If you want all that God has for you and are ready to receive the Holy Spirit that he provides for us, connect with your pastor or another mature spirit-filled follower of Jesus and ask them to pray with you to be filled. You also may simply open up your heart and ask God to fill you with his Spirit.

If you then, though you are evil, know how to give good gifts to your children, how much more will your Father in heaven give the Holy Spirit to those who ask him!
—Luke 11:13

GIFTS OF THE SPIRIT

When we're filled with the Holy Spirit, we are given spiritual gifts that deepen our walk with him and increase our effectiveness as the Church. The apostle Paul outlines for us many of the different gifts available to us as followers of Jesus:

There are different kinds of gifts, but the same Spirit distributes them. There are different kinds of service, but the same Lord. There are different kinds of working, but in all of them and in everyone it is the same God at work. Now to each one the manifestation of the Spirit is given for the common good. To one there is given through the Spirit a message of wisdom, to another a message of knowledge by means of the same Spirit, to another faith by the same Spirit, to another gifts of healing by that one Spirit, to another miraculous powers, to another prophecy, to another distinguishing between spirits, to another speaking in different kinds of tongues, and to still another the interpretation of tongues. All these are the work of one and the same Spirit, and he distributes them to each one, just as he determines.
—1 Corinthians 12:4-11

The different gifts that God gives to us through the Holy Spirit are there to build up the body of Christ. When we open up our life to be used by God, he will partner with and empower us.

Paul speaks to one of the gifts of the Holy Spirit that builds up our spirit and draws us closer to the heart of God when he notes in 1 Corinthians 14:4, "Anyone who speaks in a tongue edifies themselves." This prayer language or "tongue" is powerful for developing closeness with God and power in prayer.

YIELD, BUT DON'T STALL

Although the Holy Spirit is present to lead and guide believers, God has empowered and commissioned us to take dominion on earth and to fulfill what he's spoken to us in his Word. We don't need to sit around and wait for the Holy Spirit to tell us to do what is already written in the Bible.

Take a yielded posture that says, "I'm going hard after the purpose of God, but I'm keeping my heart sensitive to hear and adjust if the Holy Spirit speaks to me." Take time daily to pray in the Spirit, so you'll be equipped and emboldened to do all that Jesus wants you to!

CHAPTER CHALLENGE

STUDY IT THROUGH:
What did Jesus tell the disciples to wait for? Acts 1:4-5

In John 14:26, what is the Holy Spirit called?

What will we receive when the Holy Spirit comes? Acts 1:8

How does the Holy Spirit help us when we don't know what to pray? Romans 8:26-27

After repentance, what does Acts 2:38 say we will receive?

What does John 16:13 say the Holy Spirit will guide us into?

WALK IT OUT:
- Before you read the Bible, invite the Holy Spirit to reveal truth in the verses you're reading.
- If you haven't been baptized in the Holy Spirit like the Bible describes, reach out to your pastors and ask them to pray with you to receive this baptism.
- If you've already been filled with the Holy Spirit, be intentional about using the spiritual gifts the Holy Spirit has given you.

CHAPTER 5

THE CHURCH

I will put together my church, a church so expansive with energy that not even the gates of hell will be able to keep it out.

—Matthew 16:18 (MSG)

When individual followers of Jesus come together, we are called the Church. As a part of the Church, we find our community and our mission. I love the way Ephesians 1:20-22 reads in *The Message* version; it gives us one of the best visuals of the purpose and potential of the Church:

All this energy issues from Christ: God raised him from death and set him on a throne in deep heaven, in charge of running the universe, everything from galaxies to governments, no name and no power exempt from his rule. And not just for the time being, but forever. He is in charge of it all, has the final word on everything. At the center of all this, Christ rules the church. The church, you see, is not peripheral to the world; the world is peripheral to the church. The church is Christ's body, in which he speaks and acts, by which he fills everything with his presence.
—Ephesians 1:20-22 (MSG)

IN COMMUNITY

God designed us as humans to need each other; we're better together. We're designed to do life in community with other people. The Bible commonly points to the power of community:

Two are better than one, because they have a good return for their labor: If either of them falls down, one can help the other up. But pity anyone who falls and has no one to help them up.
—Ecclesiastes 4:9-10

The Bible also speaks to the value of consistently coming together as the Church and reminds us to stay faithful in being together as a church.

And let us consider how we may spur one another on toward love and good deeds, not giving up meeting together, as some are in the habit of doing, but encouraging one another—and all the more as you see the Day approaching.
—Hebrews 10:24-25

ON MISSION

Ephesians shows us that Jesus has a purpose and a plan to accomplish on earth. When we move past just following Jesus on our own to connecting with other believers in his larger Church, we become a part of the larger mission that God is accomplishing on the planet.

The Church is on a mission to extend the message of salvation through Jesus until the whole world knows.

BE THE CHURCH

We don't just "go to church," we must *be* the Church. Now technically, the place we go weekly to grow, worship God, and encourage each other *is* called church. Yet, it's also about "being" the Church every day of our life.

As followers of Jesus, gathering with other believers is essential for preparing us to *be* the Church, but it should not be our total spiritual experience. If all we are doing is attending a church service once a week, but not living for Jesus and extending the reach of his presence beyond Sunday, then we're not fully following Jesus.

There is power when we come together. We are the body of Christ: the extension of Jesus' heart and purpose on earth.

GETTING CONNECTED

One of the surest ways to keep our life healthy and connected to Jesus is by surrounding ourselves with other growing followers of Jesus. This is why getting involved with a local group of Christians is so essential and beneficial to our life.

The accountability and camaraderie that we have with other followers of Jesus is something pretty special. As the Church, we are called to reach and love the community we've been placed in, which is why most churches will have community outreach programs that are great to get connected with.

Another opportunity for growth can be found in joining a connect group. This is usually a smaller gathering of people from your church that goes through a Bible study together and encourages each other in a more casual and relational setting.

I know that jumping into a group of people you may not know is sometimes uncomfortable, but this smaller group setting will be invaluable in helping you learn and apply Scripture to your life. Our friendships really do make or break us, and connecting our life to other followers of Jesus is vitally important.

A CHURCH SERVICE EXPERIENCE

Each church that you participate in may have a slightly different feel or way of planning that gathering time, but here are several elements that you'll commonly experience during a church service.

Worship/Singing

Something powerful happens when we come together, worshipping and singing to God with other followers of Jesus. It may seem unnatural at first, but I highly recommend that you participate in worship; don't hold back. Jesus gave his life for us and deserves our praise and worship, along with the fact that worship is literally one of the most powerful ways to draw close to God and feel his presence.

Public Prayer

Often a pastor will lead the church in a prayer together. Don't just observe; join in and connect with God as well. Pray for the needs of those around you to be met.

Bible Teaching

One of the primary values of attending a weekly gathering is to receive good teaching from the Bible. We want to spend time reading the Bible on our own, but when we are new believers, it's important to lean in and learn from other Christians who know more about the Bible than we do.

After leaving a church service where God's Word has been taught, always ask the Holy Spirit to help you apply and put that teaching into practice so that it can have a lasting impact.

Tithing/Giving

At each church gathering, there will be an opportunity to give. The Bible calls us to give a tithe, which is 10% of all that we earn financially.

We give this for two primary reasons. First, everything we have comes from God. When we give him back a tithe or offering from what he has given us, we affirm that he is Lord of all and the source of all that we need and have. Giving is a declaration of our trust in him. Secondly, our giving funds the work of Jesus, which is led by pastors and other ministry leaders.

The Presence of God

While God's presence is always with us, there are moments while we are gathered together as the Church that we'll feel a heightened sense of God's presence. This is because we're not following a distant God, but a loving Father who desires to be with us. You can expect that when you take time to seek him and lean into his Word and presence that he'll come close and minister to you. There are so many incredible results from times like these—for example, it may mean that God gives you wisdom on a situation that you've been needing, or someone gets supernaturally healed, or you may simply receive an overwhelming peace from God to remind you that you are loved and that he's with you.

CHURCH LEADERSHIP

The Bible calls the Church a body, and Jesus is the head of that body:

And he (Jesus) is the head of the body, the church; he is the
beginning and the firstborn from among the dead, so that
in everything he might have the supremacy.
—Colossians 1:18

God also set in place other leadership roles under Jesus within the Church. These are men and women who are called specifically to encourage, strengthen, correct, and rally other believers to advance the kingdom of God forward.

So Christ himself gave the apostles, the prophets, the evangelists, the
pastors and teachers, to equip his people for works of service, so that the
body of Christ may be built up until we all reach unity in the faith and
in the knowledge of the Son of God and become mature, attaining to
the whole measure of the fullness of Christ.
— Ephesians 4:11-13

The role of the apostles, prophets, evangelists, pastors, and teachers is to strengthen, equip, and encourage us along the path of following Jesus.

In many areas of our lives, we need coaches to keep us focused and on track with our plans and goals. In a similar way, the church leaders that Jesus places in the church and in our life are there as coaches as well. The more we embrace their role in our life, the greater fruit or fulfillment we'll experience.

Some reading this book may sense a call to one of these church leadership roles. It is a tremendous honor, but requires great sacrifice.

Be responsive to your pastoral leaders. Listen to their counsel. They are
alert to the condition of your lives and work under the strict supervision
of God. Contribute to the joy of their leadership, not its drudgery. Why
would you want to make things harder for them?
—Hebrews 13:17 (MSG)

CHAPTER CHALLENGE

STUDY IT THROUGH:
What does the Bible say that each individual Christian forms collectively? 1 Corinthians 12:12-31

Who is the head and leader of the Church? Ephesians 1:22

Review some requirements for Church leaders laid out in 1 Timothy 3.

WALK IT OUT:
- If you don't already have a church service that you regularly attend, begin by finding one this week.
- Commit to attend weekly, unless you have to miss for work or vacation.
- See how your skills and gifts can be of service and get involved in the life of a church.

CHAPTER 6

SHARING YOUR FAITH

*Go home to your own people and tell them how much the
Lord has done for you, and how he has had mercy on you.*
—Mark 5:19

After Jesus was crucified and resurrected three days later, he spent
a few final moments with the disciples downloading the critical directions for the mission of the Church. As you can imagine, those last
conversations with Jesus would be crucial to understanding what was
next for his followers and ultimately all of us as his Church.

Before Jesus ascended into heaven, he gave his disciples and all
of us after them what we now call THE GREAT COMMISSION.
Jesus laid out the mission and sent them off to accomplish it. Let's
read what Jesus says in these few verses in Matthew 28:

*Then the eleven disciples went to Galilee, to the mountain where
Jesus had told them to go. When they saw him, they worshiped him;
but some doubted. Then Jesus came to them and said, "All authority
in heaven and on earth has been given to me. Therefore go and make
disciples of all nations, baptizing them in the name of the Father and
of the Son and of the Holy Spirit, and teaching them to obey everything
I have commanded you. And surely I am with you always, to the very
end of the age."*
—Matthew 28:16-20

Jesus was commissioning them to go and spread the message of
God's love, proclaiming that the grace of Jesus provides forgiveness
for our sins and brings us close to God again.

Now that the disciples had experienced the grace of God, they
were instructed to go out and share the good news with the entire

world! It's true that not all will welcome the message or be interested in it. Some may even be persecuted for sharing it, but when you've received forgiveness and grace, it's crazy to keep it to yourself.

Imagine if the whole world had an outbreak of a disease that was killing everyone, but you had discovered the antidote that totally cured you of the disease. Would you keep it to yourself? Would you share this answer? I think we all would try to tell everyone we could and distribute it to as many as possible!

In reality, that is what has happened to us. Because of sin, all of humanity has a deadly disease. I think we often forget that the eternity for someone who doesn't believe in Jesus is hell, which is a painful eternity away from the goodness of God. Yet we have the answer in Jesus; how could we not share it?

> *We love because he first loved us.*
> —1 John 4:19

Because of the love and grace of Jesus, we now get to live free and full of hope. With that new life we have been given, how can we not extend that hope to others around us? The most selfish thing we can do after receiving grace is to not share it with others.

Imagine if you had found something that provided endless joy and was completely free; wouldn't you want to share it? Wouldn't it be sad if you lived your whole life with that joy, but never shared it with those hurting around you?

It's the same with sharing the gospel. We have been radically rescued by Jesus, completely forgiven of all our sins, and now we have a hope and security of eternity with Jesus. We are blessed with all of God's amazing promises and favor; we must share our faith! I love how these verses talk about this great privilege we have in sharing our faith:

> *Therefore, if anyone is in Christ, the new creation has come:*
> *The old has gone, the new is here! All this is from God, who*
> *reconciled us to himself through Christ and gave us the ministry*
> *of reconciliation: that God was reconciling the world to himself in*
> *Christ, not counting people's sins against them. And he has*
> *committed to us the message of reconciliation.*
> —2 Corinthians 5:17-19

Jesus has commissioned us with this beautiful message of reconciliation! There is no greater message.

SHARING YOUR FAITH

So, how do we share our faith? What does it mean and how can we do it in a way that is effective? It's important to note that while it is our job to share our faith with people, we cannot force anyone to accept Jesus. Everyone must make that choice on their own.

Sharing your faith is often called "evangelism," but what does that mean and how should we go about it? In Mark 5, Jesus has just healed and forgiven a man. The man wants to come with Jesus, but Jesus gives him other instructions that I think are the best description of what it means to share your faith. Jesus said,

> *Go home to your own people and tell them how much the*
> *Lord has done for you, and how he has had mercy on you.*
> —Mark 5:19

Sharing your faith is simply telling the story of how Jesus has changed your life and helping to introduce someone to Jesus.

In the initial stages of following Jesus, you may not know all the right words to describe what has happened, but you can still tell people that you have experienced the love of God in a new way and you want them to know that love too.

LIVING YOUR FAITH

The best start to sharing your faith is to *live* your faith. Your life won't be perfect, but live your life filled with the love of God in such a way that it is attractive to people and makes them wonder what you have. As we live life, we look for moments to share about this incredible mercy and love that we've experienced so we can introduce people to Jesus.

When leading someone to Jesus, start by loving them. The Bible says that Jesus came to earth as a response to his love for us—not out of obligation. When we are sharing our faith with someone, let it be out of care, compassion, and love for him or her. This is not a religious formality or a chance to try to impress people with your spirituality.

When I was younger, I was taught how to share the gospel and lead a person to Jesus by walking them through several Bible verses. Let's look over these verses and a few key thoughts to help you in sharing your faith.

1. GOD CREATED US AND LOVES US

We are not an accident; God created us and loves us very much. Refer to the verse that almost everyone has heard at least once—John 3:16. This verse shows that God loves us enough to give his life in exchange for ours.

For God so loved the world that he gave his one and only Son, that whoever believes in him shall not perish but have eternal life.
—John 3:16

2. SIN SEPARATED US FROM HIM

Explain that sin is what separated us from God. It started with Adam and Eve and continues with us today. Sin is simply missing the mark, or disobeying God. We've all done it. Romans 3:23 describes how we've all sinned and fallen short of the standard that God has.

For all have sinned and fall short of the glory of God.
—Romans 3:23

3. OUR SIN NEEDED TO BE PAID FOR

Not only did we sin, but the cost of that sin was high. Actually, the cost of our sin toward God is so high that we deserve death. Even if we tried to repay this debt or bridge this gap caused by sin, it wouldn't be enough. This is why God sent Jesus. We deserve death, but God gives us the gift of eternal life through Jesus. Jesus paid the bill for our sins! Not only did Jesus come and pay the debt for us, he did it in advance, regardless of whether or not we accept it. He doesn't wait for us to get our life "fixed up"; he loves us right now, even in the midst of our sin.

But God demonstrates his own love for us in this: While we were still sinners, Christ died for us.
—Romans 5:8

4. GOD WANTS A RELATIONSHIP WITH US

Many people assume that God is angry, doesn't love them, or isn't interested in them. Often people feel like God is up in heaven just waiting for humans to make a mistake so he can punish us. But God absolutely proves otherwise when we see in John 3:16 that he sent his only Son to pay our debt. The next verse is awesome and shows the heart of God toward us.

For God did not send his Son into the world to condemn the world, but to save the world through him.
—John 3:17

5. DECIDING TO FOLLOW JESUS

Salvation and grace through Jesus is a free gift. It is not something we earn, but something we receive. Romans 10:9-10 explains how to receive grace, forgiveness of sin, and a restored relationship with God. The verses highlight two steps: declare and believe. We must *declare* that Jesus is Lord. This means that we are submitting our lives to his leadership and direction. We also have to *believe* in our hearts that Jesus died and was raised to life for us.

If you declare with your mouth, "Jesus is Lord," and believe in your heart that God raised him from the dead, you will be saved. For it is with your heart that you believe and are justified, and it is with your mouth that you profess your faith and are saved.
—Romans 10:9-10

6. PRAYING THE PRAYER OF SALVATION

Oftentimes we get nervous about this part because we might assume that a pastor is more qualified to pray or that there is an exact formula to follow. Actually, it's really simple and anyone can lead a person through this.

The prayer of salvation is basically a paraphrase of the verses in Romans that were just mentioned. It's about declaring and believing. When you ask the person you're talking with if they are ready to make the decision to follow Jesus, and they say yes, then have them repeat a simple prayer after you. Here is an example:

"God, I know you love me. I also know I've sinned and I'm sorry. Jesus, I believe that you died on the cross for my sin and you were raised again to give me life. I turn from my sin and return to you and receive your free gift of salvation. Today I declare you are my Lord, and I choose to follow you, Jesus, with everything that I am. Amen."

INVITING AND BRINGING

In addition to telling people about how Jesus has changed your life, another great way for people to encounter Jesus is by inviting them to come to a church service or event with you. Often this can be an effective, disarming way for them to see and hear more about Jesus while being introduced to a community of loving Jesus followers. Invite, and bring as many as you can to a church gathering with you. It's a powerful way to introduce people to Jesus.

THEY SAID YES, NOW WHAT?

A final note about the second half of the Great Commission: First, we are to go and tell people about Jesus, but secondly, we are to show and teach new Christians how to live according to the Bible. This is called discipleship. Discipleship is simply showing someone how to follow Jesus.

We don't have to be experts to show others how to follow Jesus. I'll talk more about how to disciple someone in our final chapter.

Leading someone to Christ and then showing them how to become a devoted follower of Jesus is the most fulfilling experiences that we have as a Christian.

CHAPTER CHALLENGE

STUDY IT THROUGH:
How are we saved? Ephesians 2:8-9

_____

What will the Holy Spirit empower us to do? Acts 1:8

_____

What is it about God that leads people to turn to him? Romans 2:4

_____

How did God often validate the gospel? Acts 14:3

_____

WALK IT OUT:
- Pray for your city to be saved.
- Share your faith this week.
- Invite someone to come with you to church.

CHAPTER 7

LOVING PEOPLE

As I have loved you, so you must love one another.
—John 13:34

As we finish this study on following Jesus, I can't think of a better way to wrap it up than by talking about love—which is the essence of our Savior.

The Bible says in 1 John 4:8 that "God is love." Love is such a powerful force on the earth. Every time we love someone, we display the very heart and nature of the Savior we follow. Nothing is more attractive than love. In the first chapter we read about Jesus telling us that the greatest and most important commandment is to love God with all that we are—but then he also says:

And the second is like it: "Love your neighbor as yourself."
—Matthew 22:39

Jesus reminds us that everything comes down to loving God and loving people. Genuine love is the primary distinguishing characteristic of a follower of Jesus.

A new command I give you: Love one another. As I have loved you, so you must love one another. By this everyone will know that you are my disciples, if you love one another.
—John 13:34-35

Jesus says, "As I loved you, so you *must* love one another." We often feel like love has to be deserved before it's given. But as someone who has received the unbelievable grace and love of God, how can we not extend love to others?

FORGIVE FREELY

Forgiveness is a hallmark of Christianity because it's a hallmark of Jesus. Jesus forgave us, so we must forgive others when they sin against us. Many people live crippled lives because they withhold forgiveness. Jesus tells a story about a man who has so much debt he'd never be able to repay it. The king forgives all the debt and sets him free. Then he goes and throws his friend in prison over a small amount of debt. The king is angry and replies,

I canceled all that debt of yours because you begged me to. Shouldn't you have had mercy on your fellow servant just as I had on you?
—Matthew 18:32-33

Someone may owe you because of what they've done or haven't done to you, but nothing compares to the forgiveness that Jesus has extended to us. God expects us to cancel the debt or the offenses of others, just like Jesus did for us.

LOVE IN ACTION

Little children (believers, dear ones), let us not love [merely in theory] with word or with tongue [giving lip service to compassion], but in action and in truth [in practice and in sincerity, because practical acts of love are more than words].
—1 John 3:18 (AMP)

Our human nature tends to be selfish and self-centered, but God calls on us to live a life of love. Love is so much more than a feeling. Love is sacrifice; love is considering the needs of others before your own. Love may begin with words, but must go beyond words to action.

Most of the time loving your neighbor as yourself will translate into giving of yourself in some way. It may be through your time, your money, or your wisdom. God himself went beyond words when he showed us his love on the cross. John 3:16 reminds us that God so loved that he GAVE.

"WE ARE NEVER MORE LIKE JESUS
THAN WHEN WE LOVE."

As we follow Jesus, let's give ourselves fully to loving God and allowing the love of God to flow through us to the world around us. God is passionately pursuing the people around you; allow God to love them through your life. Following Jesus is a life of love. Love calls us to reach out to meet the needs of the world around us, and love compels us to lead people to the only love that really satisfies— the love of Jesus!

Follow the way of love.
—1 Corinthians 14:1

CHAPTER CHALLENGE

STUDY IT THROUGH:
What does love cover? 1 Peter 4:8

_____

Did God wait for us to get it right before he loved us? Romans 5:8

_____

Whose interests are you supposed to consider first? Philippians 2:3-4

_____

WALK IT OUT:
- Take time today to thank God for his great love for you!
- Take time to think of people who have hurt you and choose to forgive them today.
- Consider someone who needs your help. What can you do? Is there a local outreach that you could give to or volunteer for in order to show the love of Jesus?

IT'S YOUR TURN

How, then, can they call on the one they have not believed in? And how can they believe in the one of whom they have not heard? And how can they hear without someone preaching to them?
—Romans 10:14

A disciple is a follower of Jesus, someone committed to following him and his ways. After reading this book, you're well on your way as a disciple or follower of Jesus.

In an earlier chapter, we talked about the call to share our faith and lead people to Jesus. Once they respond and accept Jesus, they then need to be discipled; they need to be shown how to follow Jesus.

This is the second half of the Great Commission that Jesus issues in his final instructions to his disciples. First we go into all the world with the message, then we must teach and show new believers how to walk out this new life in Jesus—this life of love.

DISCIPLESHIP IS KEY

One of the parables that Jesus teaches is about a farmer who is planting seeds in the ground. Jesus explains that the seeds represent the Word of God and the different soils represent the hearts of people. The condition of the soil determines the growth of the seed. Discipleship is essential in helping new believers receive and allow the seed of God's Word to grow until they are strong, mature believers.

Discipleship insulates a new believer from the enemy's attack, and helps their roots go deep enough to weather the storms. If a new convert doesn't get roots down deep, they are at greater risk of falling away.

But since they have no root, they last only a short time.
When trouble or persecution comes because of the word,
they quickly fall away.
—Mark 4:17 (emphasis added)

IT'S YOUR TURN

Now that you've been shown some initial and essential steps in following Jesus, it's time to pass them along to someone else.

I want to encourage and challenge you to personally respond to the call of Jesus to make disciples. Discipleship isn't just the role of the apostle, prophet, evangelist, pastor, and teacher; it's the role of every believer. You may not feel ready to disciple someone else yet, but with the Holy Spirit, the Bible, and this book, I'm confident that you'll do great. A new follower of Jesus is just waiting for someone to come alongside them and show them a few first steps in this journey.

FOLLOW ME

When Jesus called the original disciples, he simply said, "Follow me." This really is the foundation of what it means to disciple someone. Discipleship is teaching someone up close as you follow Jesus, not just telling someone what to do from a distance. The apostle Paul also understood this and gives us another snapshot into discipleship:

Follow my example, as I follow the example of Christ.
—1 Corinthians 11:1

You don't have to have all of the answers or have a degree in theology to disciple someone. The best way to disciple a person is to invite them into your world and show them how to follow Jesus. This can be accomplished both by example and by using the biblical principles that are highlighted in this book.

HOW TO DISCIPLE A NEW BELIEVER

Making a disciple of Jesus can be broken into three phases:

CHOOSE

The first step is to identify who you will disciple. You can disciple someone you've personally led to the Lord, a new acquaintance that happens to be a new believer, or you could ask a pastor at your church if they can connect you with someone to disciple.

Note: The person you choose doesn't have to be brand new to following Jesus. Often people have chosen to follow Jesus years earlier but have never been shown how to do it.

LEAD

This is the part where you show them how to follow Jesus by allowing them to see your personal example and by guiding them through the fundamentals of following Jesus.

The reason I wrote this book was to provide a quick reference guide for discipleship. I'd encourage you to set weekly meetings with the new disciple for five to eight weeks, allowing yourselves to work through *Following Jesus*. Setting a meeting will help you stay consistent in helping them walk out their new faith.

DISCIPLESHIP MEETING EXAMPLE

Purpose:
- Give them the essentials of how to follow Jesus.
- Support them in their new journey in following Jesus.
- Provide an intentional space to pray and ask questions.

Meeting Duration:
- Five to eight weeks—at least once a week.

- Meetings can be as short or as long as you want, but try to create space for both relational connection and the teaching element.

Sample Meeting Agenda:
- Spend time together.
- Invest in them relationally.
- Both of you read that week's chapter from this book ahead of time if possible or during your meeting.
- Answer or help them find the answers to any questions that they have from the chapter or just from their day-to-day life of following Jesus.
- Answer the additional study questions together. (If you have time.)
- Encourage them to do the challenges.
- Pray with them each week.

Supplies:
- Bible, or use Bible.com
- *Following Jesus* book (paperback or on digital reader)
- Coffee (or whatever will create more of a social environment)
- You may not have all of the answers, but here are a few places to find the answers:
- o   Your pastor
- o   biblegateway.com
- o   blueletterbible.com
- o   Another mature Christian

RELEASE

How long do we commit to the discipleship process with someone? It will vary depending on the individual. God may bring someone into your life that you encourage and disciple for years to come, but that would be rare. Begin with the idea of helping an individual with the initial steps when following Jesus, and see what God does from there.

The full circle and goal of discipleship is that you show a new believer how to follow Jesus, they lead someone new to Jesus, and then they show that new person how to follow Jesus. The cycle repeats until the whole world is reached with the good news about grace and life in Jesus.

Once you've taken them through this book, encourage them to do the same with someone else. You never know the eternal impact that will happen as you make and then release disciples.

Jesus invited the disciples to follow him, but promised to make them fishers of other people. So Jesus' goal wasn't just to reach them, but also to reach others through them. It's as true for you and me as it was for the original twelve disciples. Jesus has reached us, and now together with him, we'll reach the world!

LET THE JOURNEY BEGIN. . .

As we wrap up our time together, I want to remind you to continue in what you've learned and to do so more and more.

Following Jesus is an incredible lifetime of experiences, each building on the next. Continue to walk with Jesus, taking one step at a time, and invite as many as you can on the journey. I'm praying for you, and God is with you!

We instructed you how to live in order to please God, as in fact
you are living. Now we ask you and urge you in the Lord Jesus to
do this more and more.
—1 Thessalonians 4:1

FOLLOWING JESUS EXTRAS

Discover all that God has for you with our complimentary
video guides and devotionals.
FOLLOWINGJESUSBOOK.COM/EXTRAS

CHAPTER ANSWER KEY

CHAPTER 1 | PRAYER & WORSHIP

- Q: What does the Bible say about prayer and thankfulness?
  1 Thessalonians 5:16-18
  A: Pray always, be thankful in every situation

- Q: What does God ask us to pray for? Psalm 2:8
  A: Ask for the nations

- Q: How should we pray? Luke 18:1-8
  A: Be persistent and never quit

- Q: What does Jesus say about fasting? Matthew 6:16-18
  A: Do it privately and in prayer; for God to see, not others

- Q: Who are we to worship? Luke 4:8
  A: The Lord God

- Q: What does Psalm 96:1-10 say that the Lord is worthy of?
  A: Worship, praise, glory

CHAPTER 2 | THE BIBLE

- Q: What does Hebrews 4:12 and 2 Timothy 3:16 say the
  Bible is?
  A: Living and active

- Q: What does 2 Timothy 3:16-17 say the Bible is used for?
  A: Teaching, rebuking, correcting, and training in
  righteousness

- Q: What does Psalm 119:130 say that the Word of God
  brings into your life?
  A: The unfolding of your Word brings life

- Q: How do we live a pure life? Psalm 119:9
  A: By living according to your Word

- Q: What does Psalm 119:4 say about God's commands?
  A: They are to be fully obeyed

CHAPTER 3 | WATER BAPTISM

- Q: What did Jesus do before he began his public ministry? Matthew 3:13-16
  A: Water baptized by John
- Q: What are the two things we're called to do in response to the gospel? What will we receive? Acts 2:38
  A: Repent, be baptized, and receive the Holy Spirit
- Q: What accompanies believing? Mark 16:16
  A: Water baptism
- Q: When we are water baptized, who does Jesus say that we should be baptized in the name of? Matthew 28:19
  A: Baptize in the name of God (Father), Son (Jesus), Holy Spirit

CHAPTER 4 | THE HOLY SPIRIT

- Q: What did Jesus tell the disciples to wait for? Acts 1:4-5
  A: The promised Holy Spirit
- Q: In John 14:26, what is the Holy Spirit called?
  A: The helper
- Q: What will we receive when the Holy Spirit comes? Acts 1:8
  A: You will receive power
- Q: How does the Holy Spirit help us when we don't know what to pray? Romans 8:26-27
  A: The Spirit prays for us and helps us
- Q: After repentance, what does the Acts 2:38 say we will receive?
  A: Repent, be baptized, and receive the Holy Spirit

- Q: What does John 16:13 say the Holy Spirit will guide us into?
  A: All truth

CHAPTER 5 | THE CHURCH

- Q: What does the Bible say that each individual Christian forms collectively? 1 Corinthians 12:12-31
  A: The Church
- Q: Who is the head and leader of the Church? Ephesians 1:22
  A: Jesus

Review some requirements for Church leaders laid out in 1 Timothy 3.

CHAPTER 6 | SHARING YOUR FAITH

- Q: How are we saved? Ephesians 2:8-9
  A: By grace you have been saved
- Q: What will the Holy Spirit empower us to do? Acts 1:8
  A: Brings power to be his witness
- Q: What is it about God that leads people to turn to him? Romans 2:4
  A: The kindness of God
- Q: How did God often validate the gospel? Acts 14:3
  A: Through signs and wonders, miracles

CHAPTER 7 | LOVING PEOPLE

- Q: What does love cover? 1 Peter 4:8
  A: A multitude of sins

- Q: Did God wait for us to get it right before he loved us? Romans 5:8
  A: No, he loved us while we were sinners

- Q: Whose interests are you supposed to consider first? Philippians 2:3-4
  A: The needs and interests of others

NOTES

NOTES

NOTES

NOTES

NOTES

NOTES